FOR MY LOVES
DADDO, MOO MOO & BOO BOO

GRUMBLE

))

RUMBLE

Sarah, thank you for your adorable characters, amazing illustrations and endless patience. You made these books truly special.

Thanks again to Judy and Steph for your editorial help and, of course, Dave, for always inspiring me.

Text Designed by: Steph Mackie

Website: littlebellymonster.com   Email: books@littlebellymonster.com

Publisher's Notes:
This cookbook requires adult supervision and is not meant for children to do on their own. The publisher cannot accept liability for any resulting injury, damage or loss to persons or property, however they may arise.

YAWN!

Good morning.
It's me again,
Little Belly Monster!

Do you know
what a belly
monster dreams
about at night?

BREAKFAST!

Yummy,
get-up-and-go
breakfast.

But there are
so many good
choices to fill my
hungry belly.

What should I eat
to get the day
started?

GRUMBLE

RUMBLE

FRENCH TOAST!

That's a great idea!
I can help make it, too.

And with a little help
from a grown up,
so can you.
Come on,
I'll show you!

First,
we **ALWAYS**
start by washing
our hands.

Then,
we get **ALL** the
ingredients
together.

For the French toast, we'll need...

**thick slices of
whole wheat bread**

2 eggs

1/4 cup (60 mL) of milk

**1/4 teaspoon (1.25 mL)
of vanilla extract**

& canola cooking spray

Next, we get our favorite toppings. I like...

cinnamon

blueberries

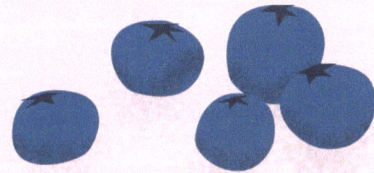

raspberries

& real maple syrup

Mmm... I can hardly wait!

2 eggs

Now we can start.
First, crack 2 eggs
into a baking pan.
Be careful not to get
any shells in there!

1/4 cup (60 mL) of milk

Pour the milk
in with the eggs.

1/4 teaspoon (1.25 mL) of
vanilla extract

Add vanilla extract
to give it a little
sweetness.

Then mix the
ingredients
together with a
fork, until it's one
light yellow colour.

SPRAY

CANOLA

OIL

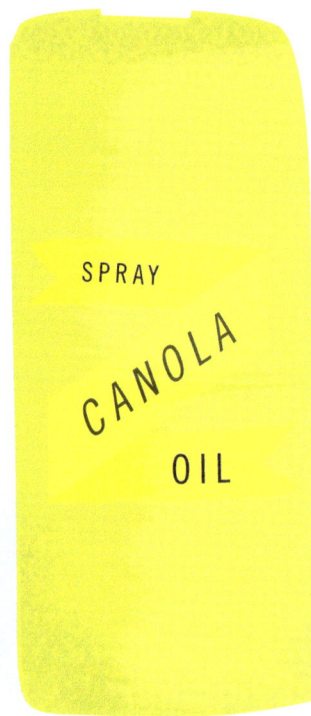

canola cooking spray

We're getting closer. But next, we need to spray canola oil✚ on a baking sheet, so the bread doesn't stick when we bake it.

✚ SAFETY: Mummo Belly sprays the canola oil on for me.

thick slices of whole wheat bread

Now, we take thick slices of whole wheat bread. Place them side by side in the egg mix, then count to 10 slowly.

1...
2...
3...

CINNAMON

OR

cinnamon

Turn the bread over and
count to 10 again.

... 8, 9, 10

Put eggy pieces of bread
on the baking sheet, until
all the egg mix is gone.

Then sprinkle*
cinnamon on top.

*SPRINKLE means drop a little bit at a time, all around.

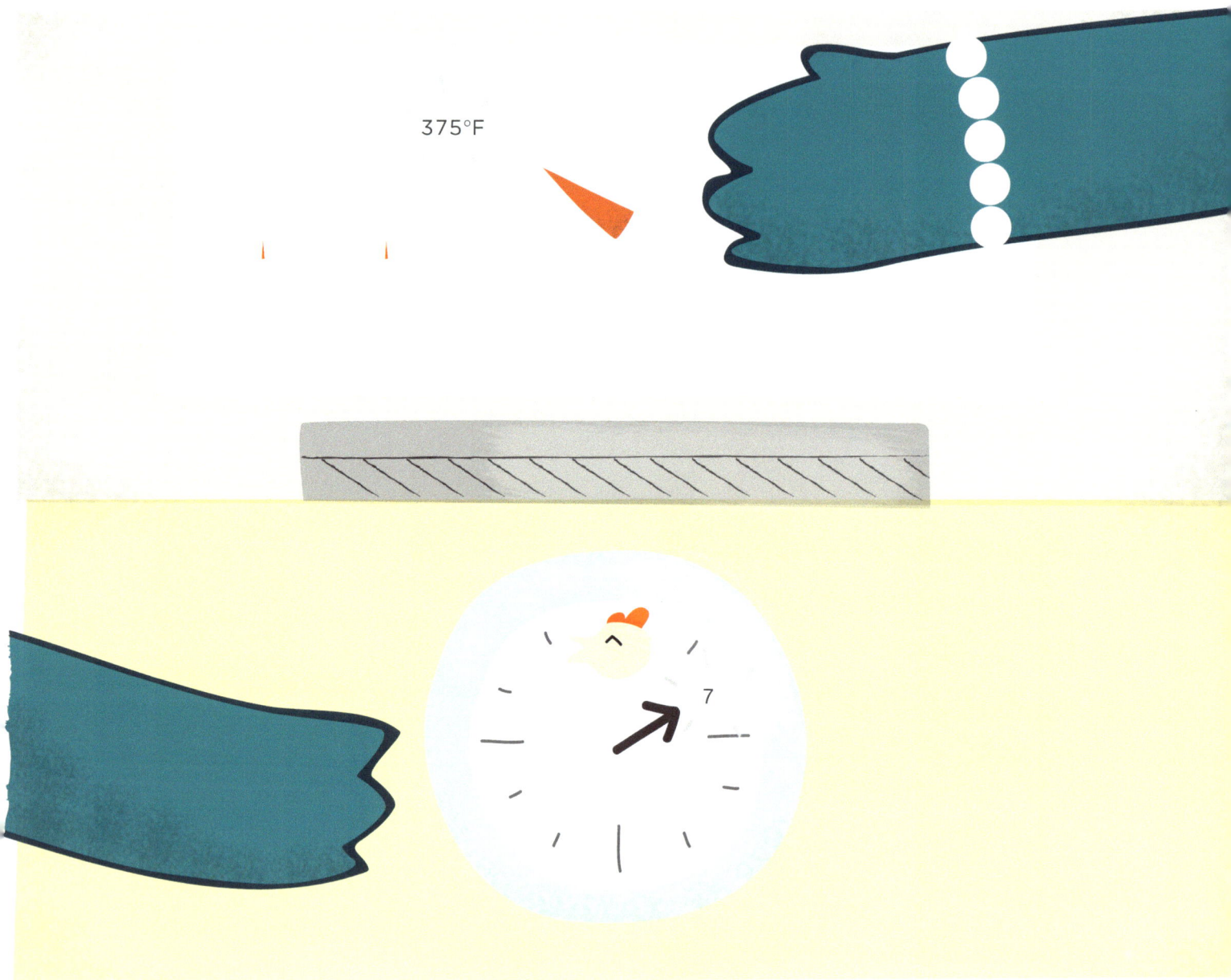

Hot oven at 375°F/190°C

375°F

for 7 minutes

Now we bake it!
Mummo Belly puts
it in the hot oven✚
for me. We wait
for 7 minutes.

**SNIFF,
SNIFF
MMM...**

Next, Mummo Belly carefully takes the baking sheet out of the oven. She flips the toast over.

Mummo sprinkles more cinnamon.

And puts it back in the oven✚ for another 6 to 10 minutes, or until the bread is a little crispy.

✚ SAFETY: The baking sheet's too hot to touch!

blueberries and raspberries

When it's all ready, Mummo puts the warm toast on a plate for me. We add blueberries and raspberries on top. Try not to eat them all first!

SLURP

SMACK

real maple syrup

Almost done.
Just pour a
little maple syrup
over it.

AND THEN...

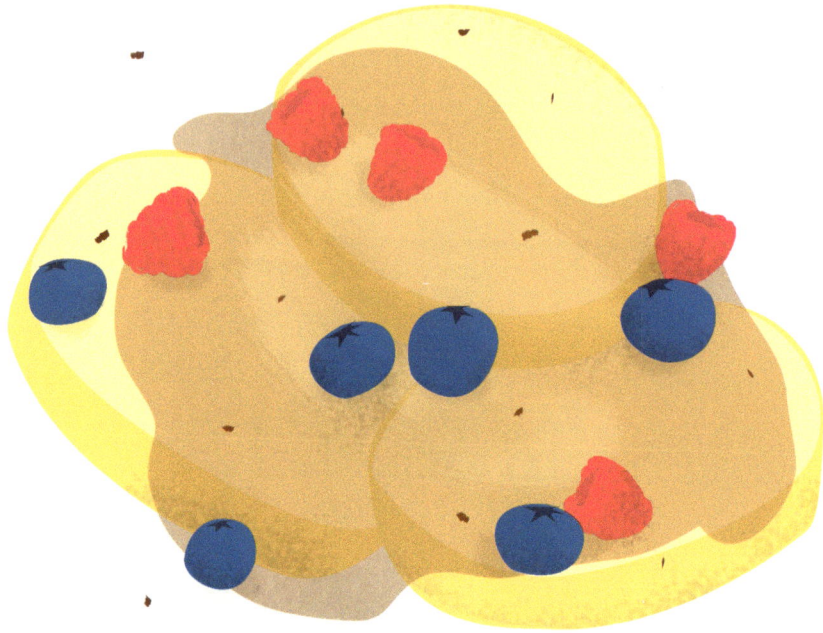

FRENCH TOAST!

WE EAT!

Mmm...

LITTLE BELLY MONSTER FRENCH TOAST!

CHOMP

CHOMP

CHOMP

That was tasty.
Thanks for helping
me make a delicious
breakfast.

SO...

what are we going
to make for lunch?

BURP

EXCUSE ME.

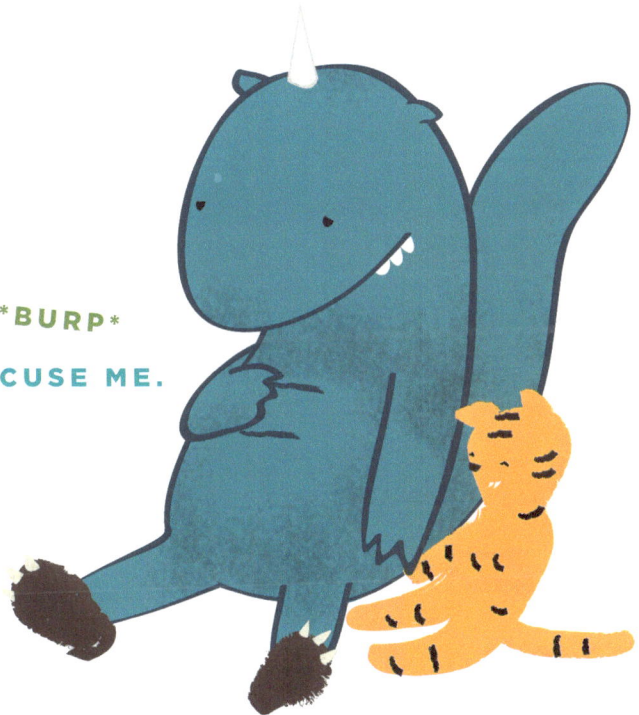

If you want to try something different, you can use other kinds of breads or change up the fruit and toppings.

BREAD

A loaf bread, like French baguette, Italian loaf or Challah bread, that can be thickly cut.

FRUIT

Add strawberries, peaches, bananas, kiwis or mangoes. Try it with one or more of these. Mmm...

TOPPINGS

Instead of real maple syrup, you can eat it plain, or with a little butter or jam. Delicious!

And, if you don't eat all the French toast, put some in the fridge or freezer and reheat them in the toaster another day.

DON'T FORGET THE YUMMY FRUIT!

SHOPPING LIST

- [ ] **WHOLE WHEAT BREAD (FOR THICK SLICES)**

- [ ] **EGGS**

- [ ] **MILK**

- [ ] **VANILLA EXTRACT**

- [ ] **CINNAMON**

- [ ] BLUEBERRIES
- [ ] RASPBERRIES
- [ ] REAL MAPLE SYRUP
- [ ] CANOLA COOKING SPRAY

Eat with you again soon!

www.ingramcontent.com/pod-product-compliance
Lightning Source LLC
LaVergne TN
LVHW072104070426

835508LV00003B/262